AIRBNB SUCCESS AWAITS:

The Blueprint For A Lucrative Startup

Dack Douglas

Icon Publications Limited

CONTENTS

INTRODUCTION

Welcome to "Airbnb Success Awaits: The Blueprint For A Lucrative Startup." This book is your comprehensive guide to starting and running a successful Airbnb business from scratch. Whether you're a property owner looking to maximize your rental income or an aspiring entrepreneur eager to enter the booming sharing economy, this book will provide you with valuable insights, practical tips, and step-by-step strategies to launch and grow your Airbnb venture.

AIRBNB SUCCESS AWAITS: THE BLUEPRINT FOR A LUCRATIVE STARTUP

TABLE OF CONTENTS

CHAPTER 1: UNDERSTANDING THE AIRBNB PHENOMENON

1a. The Rise Of The Sharing Economy And Its Impact On Travel

The surge of the sharing economy has significantly reshaped the landscape of travel, and in turn, redefined the Airbnb phenomenon. As travelers increasingly seek authentic and personalized experiences, Airbnb has thrived as a platform that connects them with unique and local accommodations, fostering a sense of belonging in unfamiliar places. The sharing economy's collaborative ethos has not only empowered individual hosts to monetize their spare spaces but also allowed travelers to immerse themselves in diverse cultures, breaking away from traditional, cookie-cutter hotel stays. This symbiotic relationship between the sharing economy and Airbnb has propelled the platform's growth, making it a prominent player in the travel industry, revolutionizing the way people explore the world.

1b. Airbnb's Role And Significance In The Accommodation Industry

Airbnb has emerged as a transformative force in the accommodation industry, redefining the very essence of travel lodging. By offering a vast array of unique and personalized accommodations, ranging from quaint cottages to luxurious penthouses, Airbnb has unlocked the doors to a world of experiential travel. Its role goes beyond being a mere booking platform; it has become a gateway to immersive journeys, allowing travelers to savor the authenticity of local cultures and communities.

In doing so, Airbnb has challenged the dominance of traditional hotels and introduced a paradigm shift, where hospitality is no longer confined to commercial establishments but extends to the homes and hearts of hosts worldwide. The significance of Airbnb lies not only in its economic impact but also in its ability to forge meaningful connections between travelers and hosts, shaping the way people explore, understand, and appreciate the world around them.

1c. Benefits And Challenges Of Starting An Airbnb Business

Starting an Airbnb business can be a rewarding venture, offering various benefits and presenting its fair share of challenges. On the positive side, it allows hosts to capitalize on underutilized spaces, generating supplemental income and potentially turning a passion for hospitality into a profitable endeavor. The platform's vast global reach provides access to a diverse pool of travelers, fostering cultural exchange and meaningful connections. Moreover, running an Airbnb business often grants hosts the flexibility to set their own rules and schedules, enabling them to manage their space on their terms.

However, like any entrepreneurial pursuit, there are challenges to navigate. Ensuring a consistent stream of bookings can be demanding, requiring hosts to maintain competitive pricing, attractive listings, and stellar guest reviews. Managing guest expectations and providing exceptional customer service can be time-consuming, demanding hosts to be responsive and adaptable to various traveler needs. Additionally, adhering to local regulations, tax obligations, and safety standards may pose legal and logistical challenges that necessitate careful attention and compliance.

Overall, starting an Airbnb business requires a delicate balance between seizing the opportunities it offers and addressing the obstacles it presents. By embracing the benefits while proactively tackling the challenges, hosts can cultivate a thriving and gratifying venture within the dynamic realm of the sharing economy.

* * *

CHAPTER 2: GETTING STARTED

2a. Assessing Your Property's Suitability For Airbnb

Assessing your property's suitability for Airbnb involves considering several key factors:

1. First, evaluate the location's appeal: proximity to tourist attractions, public transportation, and amenities can make it more enticing to potential guests.

2. Next, assess the property's condition and amenities, ensuring it meets basic comfort standards and offers unique selling points. A clean and well-maintained space with essential facilities enhances its desirability.

Understanding your target market is vital; tailor your listing to cater to their preferences and needs. Research the demand and pricing trends in your area to set competitive rates.

3. Additionally, consider the local regulations and legal requirements that may apply to short-term rentals, ensuring you can operate within the confines of the law.

4. Lastly, reflect on your own capacity to manage an Airbnb property. Hosting demands time and effort, from communication with guests to

maintaining the space. Assess whether you have the availability and willingness to provide excellent hospitality.

By carefully evaluating these aspects, you can gauge your property's suitability for Airbnb and set the foundation for a successful hosting experience.

2b. Setting Goals And Defining Your Target Audience

Setting goals and defining your target audience for your Airbnb business requires a thoughtful and strategic approach.

1. Start by envisioning the long-term vision for your hosting venture. Consider what you want to achieve, whether it's maximizing revenue, becoming a Superhost, or creating unforgettable guest experiences.

2. Next, break down these broader goals into specific, measurable, achievable, relevant, and time-bound (SMART) objectives. For instance, you might set a goal to increase bookings by a certain percentage within six months or earn a specific amount of positive reviews.

To define your target audience, conduct market research to understand the demographics, interests, and preferences of potential guests in your area. Consider the type of accommodation you offer and the experiences it can provide. Are you targeting budget-conscious travelers, business professionals, families, or adventure seekers?

Create guest personas to gain a deeper understanding of your ideal guests, their motivations, and pain points. This will help you tailor your listing, amenities, and communication to cater to their specific needs and preferences.

Remember to keep your goals and target audience dynamic, allowing room for adjustments as you gather more data and insights from your hosting experience. Regularly review your progress and adapt your strategies to ensure you're continuously optimizing your Airbnb business for success.

2c. Legal Considerations And Regulatory Requirements

As the sharing economy and short-term rental industry continue to evolve, new considerations and regulatory requirements have emerged for Airbnb businesses. Some of these include:

1. Local Regulations: Many cities and municipalities have implemented specific regulations governing short-term rentals. These may include zoning restrictions, licensing requirements, occupancy limits, and safety standards. Hosts must familiarize themselves with local laws and ensure compliance to avoid potential legal issues.

2. Taxation: Taxation rules for short-term rentals vary by location. Hosts may be required to collect and remit occupancy taxes or other applicable taxes to the authorities. Understanding tax obligations and keeping accurate financial records is essential for operating an Airbnb business.

3. Insurance Coverage: Traditional homeowner's insurance policies may not provide adequate coverage for short-term rentals. Hosts should explore

insurance options that specifically cater to short-term rental businesses, protecting both the property and liability aspects.

4. Data Privacy: Handling guest data, including personal information, requires adherence to data privacy regulations. Hosts must implement appropriate security measures and obtain consent when necessary to safeguard guest data.

5. Health and Safety Measures: The ongoing pandemic has led to increased attention on health and safety protocols. Hosts should prioritize cleanliness and sanitation, following best practices to ensure a safe environment for guests.

6. Accessibility and Inclusivity: Considerations for accessibility and inclusivity are gaining importance. Ensuring your property is accessible to all guests and promoting inclusivity in your hosting practices can enhance guest experiences.

7. Sustainability: Eco-conscious travelers are seeking sustainable accommodations. Integrating environmentally friendly practices in your hosting approach can attract eco-conscious guests and contribute to responsible tourism.

Hosts should proactively research and stay updated on the evolving regulatory landscape to maintain a compliant and successful Airbnb business. Engaging with local host communities and seeking professional advice when needed can also provide valuable insights into the new considerations and requirements that apply to their specific location.

* * *

CHAPTER 3: PREPARING YOUR PROPERTY

3a. Attracting Guests With Appealing Photos And Descriptions

To attract guests with appealing photos and descriptions of your Airbnb, consider these effective strategies:

1. Showcase Your Space Creatively: Capture high-quality photos that showcase the unique features of your property. Use natural light and highlight key selling points, such as cozy corners, stunning views, or stylish decor. Make guests envision themselves enjoying the space.

2. Set the Mood: Craft a compelling description that sets the mood and atmosphere of your Airbnb. Use descriptive language to evoke emotions and paint a vivid picture of the experience guests can expect.

3. Focus on Amenities: Highlight the amenities that make your Airbnb stand out. Whether it's a private pool, a fully equipped kitchen, or a cozy fireplace, emphasize how these features can enhance guests' stays.

4. Tell a Story: Share a captivating story about your property and its surroundings. Describe the local attractions, hidden gems, and unique experiences guests can discover during their stay.

5. Be Honest and Accurate: Transparency is crucial. Ensure that your photos and description accurately represent your property. Misleading information can lead to disappointment and negative reviews.

6. Consider Guest Reviews: Include positive guest reviews that praise specific aspects of your Airbnb. This social proof can build trust and encourage potential guests to book with confidence.

7. Personalize Communication: Respond promptly and courteously to inquiries. Personalize your responses to potential guests, addressing their specific questions and needs.

8. Offer Specials and Promotions: Consider offering limited-time specials or promotions to entice guests. This could be a discounted rate for longer stays or complimentary local experiences.

9. Be Responsive: Respond quickly to booking requests and inquiries. A prompt response indicates your commitment to excellent guest service.

10. Optimize for Mobile: Many guests browse Airbnb listings on mobile devices. Ensure that your photos and descriptions look appealing and are easily readable on various screen sizes.

By employing these strategies, you can create an enticing Airbnb listing that attracts guests and encourages them to choose your space for their next memorable getaway.

3b. Essential Amenities And Furnishings For An Exceptional Guest Experience

To create an exceptional guest experience in your Airbnb, consider providing essential amenities and furnishings that cater to the comfort and convenience of your guests:

1. Comfortable Bedding: Invest in high-quality mattresses, soft linens, and plush pillows to ensure a restful sleep experience.

2. Well-Equipped Kitchen: Stock your kitchen with essential cookware, utensils, and appliances, allowing guests to prepare their meals if they choose to do so.

3. Thoughtful Toiletries: Offer a selection of toiletries like shampoo, conditioner, body wash, and hand soap to make guests feel pampered during their stay.

4. Reliable Wi-Fi: Provide fast and reliable internet access, as many guests rely on Wi-Fi for work, entertainment, and staying connected.

5. Entertainment Options: Consider offering a range of entertainment options such as a smart TV with streaming services, board games, or books to keep guests entertained.

6. Cozy Seating Areas: Create comfortable seating areas both indoors and outdoors, allowing guests to relax and unwind during their stay.

7. Climate Control: Ensure your Airbnb has proper heating and cooling systems to maintain a comfortable environment in all seasons.

8. Ample Storage Space: Provide sufficient storage options such as closets, drawers, and luggage racks for guests to keep their belongings organized.

9. Safety Features: Install essential safety features like smoke detectors, fire extinguishers, and first aid kits to prioritize guest well-being.

10. Local Guidebook: Create a comprehensive guidebook that highlights local attractions, dining recommendations, and practical information to help

guests explore the area.

11. Cleaning Supplies: Leave cleaning supplies like a vacuum cleaner, mop, and basic cleaning agents for guests who may want to tidy up during their stay.

12. Thoughtful Extras: Consider thoughtful extras like a welcome basket with snacks, a local souvenir, or a handwritten note to add a personal touch to the guest experience.

By providing these essential amenities and thoughtful furnishings, you can elevate the comfort and enjoyment of your guests, leaving a lasting positive impression and encouraging them to return or recommend your Airbnb to others.

3c. Safety And Security Measures To Ensure Guest Satisfaction

To ensure guest satisfaction and prioritize safety and security in your Airbnb, consider implementing the following measures:

1. Keyless Entry: Install a keyless entry system that provides unique access codes for each guest. This reduces the risk of lost or duplicated keys and enhances security.

2. Security Cameras: Consider installing security cameras in common areas (e.g., entrance, living room) to deter potential intruders and enhance overall safety.

3. Emergency Information: Provide clear instructions and emergency contact details in case of any unforeseen situations or emergencies.

4. Secure Locks: Ensure all doors and windows have sturdy and secure locks to give guests peace of mind during their stay.

5. Fire Safety: Equip your Airbnb with smoke detectors, fire extinguishers, and a fire escape plan to address fire safety concerns.

6. First Aid Kit: Keep a well-stocked first aid kit easily accessible for any minor medical needs.

7. Safe Storage: Offer a safe or secure storage option for guests to keep their valuable items during their stay.

8. Regular Maintenance: Conduct regular inspections and maintenance to address any safety issues promptly.

9. Clear House Rules: Communicate clear house rules, including guidelines on using equipment, appliances, and amenities safely.

10. Exterior Lighting: Ensure well-lit pathways and entry points to enhance safety during evenings and nights.

11. Privacy Considerations: Respect guests' privacy by providing window coverings and ensuring that surveillance cameras are not placed in private areas like bedrooms or bathrooms.

12. Background Checks: Consider implementing a guest screening process, which can include verified identification and reviews from previous hosts.

13. Secure Wi-Fi: Set up a secure and password-protected Wi-Fi network for guests to safeguard their online activities.

14. Local Area Information: Provide information about any potential safety concerns or areas to avoid in the local neighborhood.

By implementing these safety and security measures, you create a welcoming and secure environment for your guests, earning their trust and ensuring a positive experience throughout their stay at your Airbnb.

* * *

CHAPTER 4: LISTING AND PRICING STRATEGY

4a. Creating An Eye-Catching Airbnb Listing

Creating an eye-catching Airbnb listing requires a combination of attention to detail and creativity to capture potential guests' attention. Here are some original tips to help you craft a standout listing:

1. Striking Photos: Invest in professional-quality photos that showcase the unique features of your property. Capture enticing angles and highlight the most appealing aspects to make a strong first impression.

2. Engaging Title: Craft a captivating title that immediately grabs attention and conveys the essence of your Airbnb. Use descriptive language and keywords relevant to your target audience.

3. Compelling Description: Write a well-crafted and engaging description that tells a story about your property. Emphasize the experience guests can expect, not just the features.

4. Highlight Key Features: Showcase your property's standout features and amenities in bullet points, making it easy for guests to see what sets your Airbnb apart.

5. Personal Touch: Add a personal touch to your listing by sharing anecdotes, recommendations, or local tips to make guests feel welcome and excited about their stay.

6. Guest Reviews: Showcase positive guest reviews that highlight the exceptional aspects of your property and the experiences guests have enjoyed during their stay.

7. Seasonal Appeal: Tailor your listing to different seasons and occasions, showcasing how your Airbnb is an ideal choice for holidays, special events, or seasonal getaways.

8. Clear Call-to-Action: Encourage potential guests to take action by including a clear call-to-action, such as "Book Now to Secure Your Stay!" or "Limited Availability – Reserve Your Dates!"

9. Virtual Tour: Consider adding a virtual tour or 360-degree photos to give guests an immersive experience of your property.

10. Consistency Across Platforms: Ensure your listing is consistent across different platforms and social media channels, maintaining a cohesive brand image.

11. Local Experiences: Mention nearby attractions, restaurants, and activities in your description to emphasize the convenience and appeal of your property's location.

12. Discounts and Special Offers: Offer limited-time discounts or special offers to incentivize potential guests to book quickly.

13. Responsive Communication: Highlight your responsiveness to inquiries and guest messages to build confidence in your guest's communication experience.

By incorporating these original elements into your Airbnb listing, you can capture the attention of potential guests, stand out among the competition, and create a lasting impression that leads to more bookings and positive reviews.

4b. Effective Pricing Strategies To Maximize Revenue And Occupancy

To maximize revenue and occupancy for your Airbnb, consider implementing these effective pricing strategies:

1. Dynamic Pricing: Utilize dynamic pricing tools that adjust your rates based on demand, seasonality, and local events. This helps optimize prices for peak periods and attract more bookings during low-demand periods.

2. Competitive Analysis: Regularly monitor the prices of similar listings in your area to ensure your rates are competitive. Adjust your pricing strategy accordingly to stand out and attract potential guests.

3. Length of Stay Discounts: Offer discounts for longer stays to entice guests to book for extended periods, increasing your overall occupancy and revenue.

4. Weekend vs. Weekday Pricing: Set different prices for weekends and weekdays, reflecting the varying demand patterns and maximizing earnings during peak times.

5. Seasonal Pricing: Adjust your rates based on seasonal demand, taking into account holidays, festivals, and local events that attract travelers to your area.

6. Last-Minute Deals: Consider offering last-minute discounts to fill gaps in your calendar and attract spontaneous travelers.

7. Early Bird Specials: Offer attractive discounts for guests who book well in advance, encouraging early reservations and ensuring steady bookings.

8. Value-Added Packages: Create appealing packages that bundle extra services or experiences, such as guided tours, spa treatments, or complimentary breakfasts, to justify higher rates.

9. Test and Monitor: Experiment with different pricing strategies and track their impact on bookings and revenue. Use data and analytics to make informed decisions about your pricing approach.

10. Minimum and Maximum Stays: Set minimum and maximum stay requirements, aligning them with popular booking patterns to optimize your occupancy.

11. Seasonal Adjustments: Consider adjusting your pricing dynamically as demand fluctuates throughout the year, reflecting the changing seasons and local events.
12. Loyalty Discounts: Reward repeat guests with exclusive discounts or special perks to encourage them to return and become loyal customers.

By implementing these original pricing strategies, you can optimize your Airbnb's revenue and occupancy, ensuring a steady flow of bookings while providing competitive rates that attract and retain guests. Regularly evaluate and refine your pricing approach to adapt to market trends and guest preferences.

4c. Utilizing Dynamic Pricing Tools And Competitor Analysis

To enhance your pricing strategy for your Airbnb business, consider utilizing dynamic pricing tools and competitor analysis:

1. Dynamic Pricing Tools: There are several dynamic pricing tools available that use algorithms and data analysis to adjust your rates in real-time based on various factors such as demand, seasonality, local events, and competitor pricing. Some popular dynamic pricing tools include Beyond Pricing, PriceLabs, and Wheelhouse.

2. Competitor Analysis: Conduct regular competitor analysis to stay informed about pricing trends in your area. Identify similar listings in your neighborhood and track their rates, booking patterns, and any special offers they may be providing. This information can help you position your pricing competitively and make informed decisions about adjusting your rates.

3. Market Research: Stay up-to-date with industry trends and local market conditions to understand the demand and supply dynamics in your area. Keep an eye on major events, holidays, and tourist seasons that might influence pricing and occupancy rates.

4. Historical Booking Data: Analyze your historical booking data to identify patterns and trends. Look for booking peaks, periods of low demand, and average length of stay to inform your pricing decisions.

5. Guest Reviews and Feedback: Monitor guest reviews and feedback to gauge guest satisfaction and the perceived value of your listing. Positive reviews can justify premium pricing, while areas of improvement may indicate opportunities to adjust your rates accordingly.

6. Airbnb Analytics: Utilize Airbnb's built-in analytics tools, such as the "Host Dashboard," to track your listing's performance, including occupancy

rates, average daily rates, and booking lead times.

7. Custom Rate Adjustments: Consider manually adjusting your rates for specific events, local festivals, or holiday periods when demand is expected to be higher. Tailor your pricing to capitalize on these peak times.

8. Seasonal Promotions: Offer seasonal promotions or limited-time discounts to attract guests during off-peak periods or to fill last-minute vacancies.

By combining these original approaches to dynamic pricing tools and competitor analysis, you can fine-tune your pricing strategy to optimize revenue and occupancy for your Airbnb business. Stay proactive in adjusting your rates based on market dynamics and guest preferences, ensuring your listing remains competitive and attractive to potential guests

* * *

CHAPTER 5: GUEST COMMUNICATION AND HOSPITALITY

5a. Effective Communication With Potential And Confirmed Guests

Effective communication is essential for your Airbnb business to build trust, provide exceptional hospitality, and ensure a positive guest experience. Here are some original tips for communicating with potential and confirmed guests:

1. Prompt Responses: Respond promptly to inquiries and booking requests. Quick and courteous replies show your attentiveness and commitment to excellent guest service.

2. Personalized Messages: Tailor your messages to each guest's specific inquiries or needs. Personalization creates a sense of connection and makes guests feel valued.

3. Clear and Detailed Information: Provide clear and detailed information about your listing, amenities, and house rules. Transparency helps set proper expectations for guests.

4. Pre-Arrival Communication: Send a pre-arrival message with important details, such as check-in instructions, parking information, and local tips, to

ensure a smooth arrival experience.

5. Thank-You Notes: Send a thank-you note to guests after their stay, expressing appreciation for choosing your Airbnb and inviting them to return in the future.

6. Professional Tone: Maintain a professional tone in your communication while also being warm and welcoming. This balance fosters a friendly yet respectful relationship with guests.

7. Multilingual Support: If your area attracts international guests, consider offering multilingual support or using translation tools to accommodate various language preferences.

8. Proactive Updates: Inform guests about any changes or updates that may affect their stay, such as construction nearby or improvements to your property.

9. Handling Feedback: Respond to guest feedback, whether positive or negative, with professionalism and a willingness to address their concerns constructively.

10. Timely Support: Offer timely support during the guest's stay, ensuring they can reach you easily if they have any questions or encounter issues.

11. Automated Messages: Use automated messages for routine communications, such as booking confirmations and check-in instructions, to streamline your communication process.

12. Guest Surveys: After guests check out, consider sending a survey to gather feedback on their experience. This information can help you identify areas for improvement and enhance your hosting practices.

By implementing these original communication practices, you can foster positive guest relationships, increase guest satisfaction, and encourage guests to leave positive reviews and recommend your Airbnb to others. Effective communication plays a vital role in building a strong reputation and driving repeat bookings for your hosting business.

5b. Providing Exceptional Customer Service Throughout The Guest Journey

To provide exceptional customer service throughout the guest journey for your Airbnb business, consider the following original strategies:

1. Warm Welcome: Create a warm and personalized welcome for guests upon their arrival. Greet them in person if possible, or leave a thoughtful welcome note and a small gesture like a welcome basket to make them feel special from the moment they step in.

2. Prompt Communication: Maintain open lines of communication and respond promptly to guest inquiries and messages. Address any questions or concerns they may have to ensure they feel heard and valued.

3. Anticipate Needs: Anticipate guest needs and go the extra mile to provide essential amenities, such as toiletries, snacks, and local guides. Understanding their preferences and preferences can enhance their experience.

4. Local Recommendations: Offer personalized local recommendations, such as restaurants, attractions, and activities, tailored to each guest's interests. This demonstrates your knowledge of the area and helps guests make the most of their stay.

5. Regular Check-ins: Check in with guests periodically during their stay to ensure everything is going smoothly. This proactive approach allows you to

address any issues promptly and make necessary adjustments.

6. Attention to Detail: Pay attention to the smallest details in your property, such as cleanliness, decor, and functionality. Creating a well-maintained and inviting space elevates the guest experience.

7. Flexibility and Accommodation: Be flexible and accommodating to guest requests whenever possible. Strive to fulfill special requests, such as early check-ins or late check-outs, to exceed expectations.

8. Problem Resolution: If an issue arises during a guest's stay, resolve it promptly and professionally. Be understanding and empathetic, offering appropriate compensation or alternative solutions to ensure guest satisfaction.

9. Farewell Gesture: Bid guests farewell with a thoughtful gesture, such as a thank-you note or a small parting gift. This leaves a lasting positive impression and encourages them to consider returning in the future.

10. Post-Stay Follow-up: After guests check out, send a follow-up message expressing gratitude for their stay and inviting them to provide feedback. Take guest feedback seriously and use it to continually improve your hosting practices.

By incorporating these original customer service strategies into your guest journey, you can create a memorable and delightful experience for your guests. Exceptional customer service fosters positive guest reviews, word-of-mouth referrals, and increased guest loyalty, ultimately contributing to the success of your Airbnb business

5c. Managing Guest Expectations And Resolving Issues Professionally

Effectively managing guest expectations and professionally resolving issues is vital for maintaining a positive reputation and ensuring guest satisfaction in your Airbnb business. Here are some original strategies to achieve this:

1. Clear Communication: Set clear expectations from the start by providing detailed and accurate information about your listing, amenities, house rules, and check-in procedures. Transparency helps guests know what to expect and reduces the likelihood of misunderstandings.

2. Prompt and Courteous Responses: Respond to guest inquiries and messages promptly and courteously. Be attentive to their needs and concerns, showing that you value their communication.

3. Set Realistic Expectations: Avoid overselling your property or promising unrealistic experiences. Be honest about your property's strengths and limitations to prevent disappointment.

4. Personalized Welcome: Provide a personalized and warm welcome to guests upon arrival, ensuring they feel comfortable and at home.

5. Active Listening: When guests raise concerns or issues, actively listen to their feedback and empathize with their perspective. Show genuine interest in resolving the matter.

6. Address Issues Proactively: If you anticipate potential issues (e.g., noise from construction nearby), communicate these to guests in advance to manage their expectations.

7. Empower Your Guests: Provide guests with the information they need to navigate their stay independently. Offer guides, manuals, and local

information to empower them to make the most of their visit.

8. Swift Resolution: Address any issues that arise during the guest's stay promptly and professionally. Take ownership of the situation and work towards a timely resolution.

9. Remain Calm and Polite: When dealing with guest complaints or challenging situations, maintain a calm and polite demeanor. Avoid getting defensive and focus on finding solutions.

10. Compensation and Apologies: If appropriate, offer compensation or apologies for legitimate inconveniences. A small gesture can go a long way in showing guests that you value their experience.

11. Follow Up: After resolving an issue, follow up with guests to ensure they are satisfied with the outcome. Express gratitude for their understanding and feedback.

12. Learn and Improve: Use guest feedback as an opportunity to learn and improve your hosting practices. Identify patterns in feedback to address recurring issues and enhance the guest experience.

By implementing these original strategies, you can manage guest expectations effectively, handle challenges professionally, and create a positive and memorable experience for your guests. This proactive approach builds trust, fosters guest loyalty, and contributes to the success and growth of your Airbnb business.

* * *

CHAPTER 6: OPTIMIZING YOUR AIRBNB PERFORMANCE

6a. Managing Availability And Booking Calendars

Managing availability and booking calendars effectively is crucial for a well-organized and successful Airbnb business. Here are some original ways to achieve this:

1. Synchronized Calendars: Use Airbnb's calendar synchronization feature to ensure that your listing's availability is up-to-date across all platforms. This prevents double bookings and ensures consistency in your calendar management.

2. Regular Updates: Regularly update your booking calendar to reflect changes in availability, such as reservations, blocked dates, or seasonal adjustments. Keeping the calendar current helps you manage bookings more efficiently.

3. Block-off Periods: Block off dates when your property is not available for bookings, such as personal use, maintenance, or any other reasons that require the property to be off the market temporarily.

4. Seasonal Pricing: Adjust your pricing and availability according to seasonal demand and local events. Optimize rates during peak times and attract guests during low-demand periods.

5. Minimum and Maximum Stay Rules: Set minimum and maximum stay requirements to control the length of bookings. This helps ensure that your calendar aligns with your hosting preferences.

6. Advance Booking Window: Determine your desired booking window in advance. For example, you may choose to accept bookings up to six months ahead or only allow last-minute reservations.

7. Buffer Time: Incorporate buffer time between bookings to allow for cleaning, restocking, and preparation for the next guest. This ensures a smooth transition between stays.

8. Instant Booking Settings: Customize your instant booking settings based on your comfort level and hosting capacity. You can choose to pre-approve guests or opt for manual approval, depending on your preferences.

9. Calendar Notifications: Enable calendar notifications to receive alerts about new bookings, inquiries, and reservation changes promptly. This helps you stay on top of your schedule and respond quickly to guests.
10. Sync with Personal Calendar: Sync your Airbnb calendar with your personal calendar to avoid any scheduling conflicts and ensure you can plan around your hosting commitments.

11. Booking Restrictions: Set booking restrictions, such as check-in and check-out days, to create a structured booking schedule that aligns with your availability.

12. Utilize Seasonal Trends: Analyze past booking patterns and seasonal trends to make informed decisions about adjusting your calendar, rates, and availability during different times of the year.

By employing these original strategies for managing your availability and booking calendars, you can streamline your operations, maintain an organized hosting schedule, and optimize your Airbnb business for success. Efficient calendar management contributes to guest satisfaction and allows you to focus on delivering exceptional hospitality experiences.

6b. Utilizing Guest Reviews And Feedback To Improve Your Business

Utilizing guest reviews and feedback is a valuable way to continuously improve your Airbnb business. Here's how you can do it effectively:

1. Regularly Monitor Reviews: Regularly check guest reviews to gain insights into their experiences and identify areas for improvement. Pay attention to both positive and negative feedback.

2. Acknowledge Positive Reviews: Respond to positive reviews with gratitude and appreciation. Show that you value guest feedback and their positive experiences.

3. Address Negative Reviews Professionally: Respond to negative reviews professionally and empathetically. Acknowledge any issues raised and demonstrate your commitment to resolving them.

4. Identify Patterns: Look for recurring themes or patterns in guest feedback. Identifying common feedback can help you address underlying issues or enhance specific aspects of your listing or hosting practices.

5. Take Action: Act on guest feedback by making necessary improvements or adjustments. Whether it's upgrading amenities, enhancing cleanliness, or

refining your check-in process, implementing changes shows that you listen to guests' concerns.

6. Guest Communication: Encourage open communication with guests during their stay, seeking feedback or suggestions to make their experience even better.

7. Learn from Constructive Criticism: Embrace constructive criticism as an opportunity for growth. Use feedback to reflect on your hosting practices and find ways to enhance the guest experience.

8. Stay Consistent: Use guest reviews as a tool to ensure consistency in the quality of your service. Strive to deliver the same level of exceptional hospitality to every guest.

9. Share Positive Changes: If you make improvements based on guest feedback, communicate these updates in your listing or welcome message. Let potential guests know that you actively listen to feedback and continuously enhance your offerings.

10. Follow Up: After implementing changes based on feedback, follow up with subsequent guests to gauge the impact of the improvements and seek their input.

11. Monitor Performance: Continuously monitor your listing's overall performance, including your review scores and guest satisfaction, to track your progress over time.

By utilizing guest reviews and feedback in this manner, you can enhance your Airbnb business, provide better guest experiences, and build a positive reputation that attracts more bookings and repeat guests. Embracing feedback as an essential part of your business development allows you to continually evolve and thrive as a successful Airbnb host

6c. Increasing Bookings Through Marketing And Promotion Techniques

Increasing bookings for your Airbnb business requires implementing effective marketing and promotion techniques. Here are some original strategies to attract more guests:

1. Optimized Listing: Create an enticing and detailed listing that showcases the unique features of your property. Use high-quality photos, engaging descriptions, and highlight the local experiences guests can enjoy.

2. Social Media Presence: Leverage social media platforms to promote your Airbnb. Share stunning photos, guest reviews, and upcoming events in your area to attract potential guests.

3. Influencer Collaborations: Partner with local influencers or travel bloggers who have a significant following. Their endorsements can introduce your Airbnb to a wider audience.

4. Special Offers and Packages: Offer exclusive promotions, discounts, or value-added packages to entice potential guests. Consider seasonal deals or discounted rates for extended stays to attract diverse travelers.

5. Targeted Advertising: Utilize online advertising platforms to target potential guests based on their interests, location, and travel preferences.

6. Guest Referral Program: Implement a guest referral program, offering incentives for guests who refer friends or family to book your Airbnb.

7. Collaborations with Local Businesses: Forge partnerships with nearby businesses such as restaurants, tour operators, or spas. Offer your guests

discounts or exclusive deals with these partners to enhance their stay experience.

8. Email Marketing: Build an email list of past guests and potential leads. Send personalized emails with updates, special offers, and exclusive promotions to keep them engaged.

9. Virtual Tours: Offer virtual tours or 360-degree photos of your Airbnb to give potential guests an immersive experience of your property.
10. Respond to Reviews: Respond to guest reviews, both positive and negative, to show your attentiveness and dedication to guest satisfaction.

11. Blogging and Content Marketing: Start a travel blog or create content related to your area's attractions and activities. This establishes you as a local expert and can attract travelers seeking authentic experiences.

12. Local Events and Festivals: Promote your Airbnb during local events and festivals by adjusting your pricing and showcasing your property's proximity to the festivities.

By employing these original marketing and promotion techniques, you can increase bookings for your Airbnb business, expand your guest reach, and position yourself as a top choice for travelers seeking memorable stays. Consistency and creativity in your marketing efforts will drive interest, boost occupancy rates, and contribute to the success of your Airbnb venture

* * *

CHAPTER 7: SCALING AND EXPANSION

7a. Scaling Up Your Airbnb Business With Multiple Properties

Scaling up your Airbnb business with multiple properties requires a strategic approach and effective management. Here are some original steps to help you achieve successful expansion:

1. Streamlined Operations: Establish efficient operational processes to handle multiple properties smoothly. Centralize tasks such as bookings, cleaning, and guest communication to maintain consistency across all listings.

2. Professional Property Management: Consider hiring a property management company or dedicated staff to oversee day-to-day operations, ensuring each property receives the attention it deserves.

3. Diversified Locations: Choose diverse locations for your properties to attract a broader range of guests and cater to different travel preferences. This enhances your market reach and reduces the risk of relying on a single location.

4. Branding and Cohesion: Create a strong brand identity for your Airbnb business, making it recognizable and trustworthy. Ensure that each property reflects your brand's values and offers a consistent guest experience.

5. Pricing Strategy: Develop a dynamic pricing strategy that considers demand, seasonality, and local events for each property. This maximizes revenue while maintaining competitive rates.

6. Digital Marketing: Invest in digital marketing to promote your expanding Airbnb business. Utilize social media, email campaigns, and targeted advertising to reach potential guests and highlight the unique features of each property.

7. Guest Loyalty Program: Implement a guest loyalty program to encourage repeat bookings across your properties. Offer rewards or exclusive perks for returning guests to foster brand loyalty.

8. Technology Integration: Utilize property management software that integrates all your listings, bookings, and communication in one place. This streamlines operations and simplifies management tasks.

9. Local Partnerships: Forge partnerships with local businesses, tour operators, or event organizers to offer exclusive guest experiences. Collaborations can enhance the value proposition of your properties.

10. Continuous Improvement: Regularly analyze performance metrics and guest feedback for each property. Use insights to identify areas for improvement and implement necessary changes.

11. Quality Control: Maintain high-quality standards across all properties to uphold your reputation and ensure guest satisfaction.

12. Financial Planning: Develop a solid financial plan to assess the costs and returns of scaling up. Consider factors such as property acquisition, management fees, and marketing expenses.

Scaling up your Airbnb business with multiple properties is an ambitious endeavor that requires careful planning, dedication, and a commitment to delivering exceptional guest experiences. By applying these original strategies, you can successfully expand your Airbnb business and create a portfolio of properties that attracts a diverse clientele and maximizes your revenue potential

7b. Hiring And Managing Staff Or Third-Party Services

When hiring and managing staff or third-party services for your Airbnb business, consider implementing these original practices:

1. Clear Job Descriptions: Create detailed job descriptions that outline responsibilities, qualifications, and expectations for each position or service you seek to hire. This helps attract the right candidates or service providers who align with your needs.

2. Thorough Screening: Conduct thorough interviews and background checks to ensure you select reliable and trustworthy staff or service providers. Verify references and assess their experience in the hospitality industry.

3. Training and Onboarding: Provide comprehensive training and onboarding for your staff or third-party services to familiarize them with your property's operations, guest expectations, and service standards.

4. Defined Roles and Responsibilities: Clearly define roles and responsibilities for each staff member or service provider to avoid confusion and ensure a smooth workflow.

5. Performance Evaluation: Implement regular performance evaluations to assess staff or service providers' performance and provide constructive feedback for improvement.

6. Communication Channels: Establish effective communication channels for staff or third-party services to address any issues or questions promptly.

7. Empowerment and Autonomy: Encourage staff or service providers to take ownership of their roles and provide opportunities for them to contribute ideas and improvements.

8. Incentives and Recognition: Offer incentives and recognition programs to motivate staff or service providers to deliver exceptional service and go above and beyond guest expectations.

9. Quality Control: Conduct periodic quality checks or mystery guest visits to assess the level of service provided by your staff or third-party services.

10. Contractor Agreements: When hiring third-party services, ensure you have clear contractor agreements that outline the scope of work, payment terms, and confidentiality clauses, where applicable.

11. Adaptability: Be flexible and adaptable in managing staff or third-party services, considering the changing needs and demands of your Airbnb business.

12. Building Relationships: Cultivate a positive and collaborative working environment, fostering strong relationships with your staff or third-party providers to build trust and loyalty.

By implementing these original practices for hiring and managing staff or third-party services, you can ensure the smooth operation of your Airbnb business and deliver exceptional guest experiences. Building a reliable and dedicated team or partnering with reputable

7c. Exploring Additional Revenue Streams And Diversification

Exploring additional revenue streams and diversification can strengthen your Airbnb business. Here are original ways to achieve this:

1. Experience Packages: Offer curated local experiences for guests, such as guided tours, cooking classes, or outdoor adventures. Partner with local experts to create unique packages that guests can book alongside their accommodations.

2. Co-Hosting: Explore co-hosting arrangements with property owners who may need assistance in managing their listings. Expand your services to handle multiple properties, generating additional revenue through co-hosting fees.

3. Extended Stays: Target business travelers or individuals seeking temporary housing by offering extended-stay options. Provide attractive discounts or special amenities for guests booking extended periods, ensuring consistent revenue flow.

4. Seasonal Decor and Themes: Tailor your listing to seasonal themes or events, attracting guests seeking holiday getaways or themed experiences throughout the year.

5. Property Upgrades: Invest in property upgrades that enhance guest experiences and justify premium pricing. Consider adding a pool, outdoor entertainment area, or unique interior features.

6. Affiliate Partnerships: Establish affiliate partnerships with local businesses, such as restaurants, shops, or tour operators. Earn commissions on guest referrals, and provide guests with exclusive discounts at partner establishments.

7. Professional Photography: Offer professional photography services to other Airbnb hosts in your area. High-quality listing photos can significantly improve booking rates, making this a valuable revenue stream.

8. Special Events and Retreats: Host special events, workshops, or wellness retreats at your property during low-demand periods. Collaborate with event organizers to attract larger groups and generate revenue beyond accommodation bookings.

9. Corporate Bookings: Attract corporate bookings by providing amenities suitable for business travelers, such as a dedicated workspace, high-speed internet, and convenient access to conference facilities.

10. Gift Certificates: Offer gift certificates that guests can purchase and use for future stays or to gift to friends and family. This generates revenue upfront and encourages repeat bookings.

11. Customized Services: Provide add-on services like grocery shopping, airport transfers, or in-house chef services to cater to guests' specific needs and preferences.

12. Virtual Experiences: Extend your hosting capabilities to virtual experiences like online workshops or virtual tours, attracting a broader audience and diversifying revenue sources.

By exploring these original ways to generate additional revenue streams and diversify your Airbnb business, you can adapt to market changes, optimize income potential, and offer diverse experiences that appeal to a wide range of guests. Embrace innovation and creativity to stay ahead in the competitive vacation rental industry.

CHAPTER 8: LEGAL, FINANCIAL, AND TAX CONSIDERATIONS

8a. Legal Compliance And Permits For Short-Term Rentals

Ensuring legal compliance and obtaining necessary permits for short-term rentals is crucial for the success and sustainability of your Airbnb business. Here are some original reasons why you should consider this aspect:

1. Legitimacy and Trust: Obtaining the required permits and complying with local regulations establishes your Airbnb business as a legitimate and trustworthy operation. Guests are more likely to book with confidence when they know you are operating within the bounds of the law.

2. Avoiding Penalties: Ignoring legal compliance can lead to severe penalties, fines, or even the shutdown of your Airbnb business. Complying with regulations helps you avoid costly legal issues and maintain a positive reputation.

3. Guest Safety and Satisfaction: Meeting legal requirements often includes safety standards and quality checks. Ensuring compliance enhances guest

safety and satisfaction, reducing the risk of accidents or negative experiences.

4. Building Good Relationships: Abiding by local regulations demonstrates respect for your community and neighbors. It helps build positive relationships with your surroundings, minimizing the potential for complaints and conflicts.

5. Insurance Coverage: Some permits may be a prerequisite for obtaining proper insurance coverage for your short-term rental property. Having insurance protects you and your guests from unforeseen incidents.

6. Enhancing Property Value: Compliance with legal regulations can positively impact the value of your property. It adds a layer of assurance for potential buyers or investors, making your property more attractive in the long run.

7. Competitive Advantage: Legal compliance can give you a competitive advantage over other short-term rental operators who may not have the required permits. It shows that you prioritize professionalism and guest safety.

8. Long-Term Viability: By addressing legal requirements and permits, you invest in the long-term viability of your Airbnb business. You can confidently operate without the fear of sudden legal complications.

9. Support Local Economy: Complying with regulations supports local governments and the broader tourism industry. It ensures that tourism revenue is contributing to the community's growth and development.

10. Responsible Hosting: Being a responsible host includes adhering to legal requirements and being accountable for your actions. It reflects your commitment to running a responsible and ethical business.

By considering legal compliance and obtaining the necessary permits for your Airbnb business, you demonstrate your commitment to being a responsible and reputable host. It safeguards your business, enhances guest experiences, and contributes positively to your community and the broader hospitality industry.

8b. Financial Management, Budgeting, And Record-Keeping

Implementing effective financial management, budgeting, and record-keeping practices is crucial for the success and sustainability of your Airbnb business. Here are some original strategies to achieve this:

1. Separate Accounts: Maintain separate bank accounts for your Airbnb business and personal finances. This segregation simplifies tracking income and expenses, making financial management more efficient.

2. Budgeting: Create a detailed budget that outlines your expected income and expenses. Consider fixed costs such as mortgage payments and utilities, as well as variable expenses like maintenance and marketing.

3. Emergency Fund: Set aside a portion of your earnings as an emergency fund to cover unexpected expenses or periods of low occupancy. Having a financial buffer provides peace of mind and ensures you can handle unforeseen challenges.

4. Expense Tracking: Use accounting software or spreadsheets to diligently track all income and expenses related to your Airbnb business. This practice helps you maintain accurate financial records for tax purposes and business analysis.

5. Tax Planning: Stay informed about tax regulations and deductions applicable to short-term rentals. Plan for tax payments throughout the year to avoid last-minute surprises during tax season.

6. Automation: Utilize financial management tools to automate tasks such as expense categorization, invoicing, and payment reminders. Automation streamlines your financial processes and saves time.

7. Pricing Analysis: Conduct regular pricing analysis to ensure your rates are competitive yet profitable. Adjust your pricing strategy based on demand, seasonality, and market trends.

8. Cost Optimization: Seek cost-saving opportunities by negotiating contracts with suppliers, using energy-efficient appliances, and exploring bulk purchasing for essential supplies.

9. Debt Management: If you have loans or mortgages related to your Airbnb business, manage debt responsibly. Prioritize repayments and avoid accumulating unnecessary debt.

10. Regular Financial Reviews: Set aside time for regular financial reviews to evaluate your financial performance, identify areas for improvement, and plan for future investments or expansions.

11. Professional Advice: Seek advice from financial experts or accountants who specialize in short-term rental businesses. Their insights can help you make informed financial decisions and optimize your financial strategy.

12. Financial Goals: Establish clear financial goals for your Airbnb business, such as revenue targets or return on investment (ROI). Regularly assess your progress towards these goals and make necessary adjustments.

By implementing these original financial management practices, you can maintain a healthy financial foundation for your Airbnb business, make informed decisions, and ensure long-term financial

8c. Understanding Tax Obligations And Optimizing Deductions

Understanding tax obligations and optimizing deductions for your Airbnb business is essential to ensure compliance and maximize your tax benefits. Here's an original approach to achieving this:

1. Educate Yourself: Take the time to educate yourself about the specific tax regulations and obligations that apply to short-term rental businesses in your area. Familiarize yourself with tax laws, allowable deductions, and reporting requirements.

2. Seek Professional Advice: Consider consulting with a tax professional who specializes in short-term rentals or small businesses. Their expertise can help you navigate complex tax matters and identify deductions you may have overlooked.

3. Separate Business Expenses: Maintain clear separation between personal and business expenses. Deduct only those expenses that directly relate to your Airbnb business to avoid tax discrepancies.

4. Keep Detailed Records: Maintain detailed and organized records of all income and expenses related to your Airbnb business. This practice ensures accuracy during tax preparation and helps support your deductions.

5. Understand Depreciation: Understand the concept of depreciation for items such as furniture, appliances, and improvements to your property.

Depreciation allows you to deduct a portion of the cost over several years.

6. Utilize Deductions: Take advantage of deductions allowed for short-term rental businesses, such as mortgage interest, property taxes, cleaning fees, supplies, maintenance, and utilities.

7. Track Home Office Expenses: If you have a dedicated space in your home for managing your Airbnb business, track home office expenses that may be eligible for deduction, like a portion of your rent or mortgage.

8. Timing Matters: Be aware of the timing of income and expenses. Properly categorize income and expenses in the appropriate tax year to optimize deductions and accurately reflect your financial situation.

9. Quarterly Estimated Taxes: If you anticipate owing a significant amount of taxes, consider making quarterly estimated tax payments to avoid penalties and manage your tax liability throughout the year.

10. Periodic Reviews: Regularly review your financial records and tax-related documents to identify opportunities for tax optimization and ensure compliance with changing tax laws.

11. Stay Informed: Stay informed about updates or changes in tax laws that may affect short-term rental businesses. Being aware of any legislative changes allows you to adjust your tax strategy accordingly.

12. Document Improvements: Keep records of any significant property improvements made throughout the year, as they may qualify for additional deductions or affect your property's tax basis.

By adopting this original approach to understanding tax obligations and optimizing deductions, you can confidently navigate tax season, minimize your tax liability, and make the most of available deductions for your Airbnb business. Being proactive about tax planning ensures a smooth financial journey and maximizes your return on investment.

CHAPTER 9: NAVIGATING CHALLENGES AND MITIGATING RISKS

9a. Dealing With Difficult Guests And Resolving Conflicts

Dealing with difficult guests and resolving conflicts in your Airbnb business requires a tactful and professional approach. Here's an original strategy to handle such situations effectively:

1. Active Listening: When faced with a difficult guest or conflict, practice active listening to understand their concerns fully. Let the guest express their perspective without interruption, and show empathy to validate their feelings.

2. Remain Calm and Respectful: Maintain a calm and respectful demeanor throughout the interaction. Avoid getting defensive or confrontational, as it can escalate tensions further.

3. Address Issues Promptly: Respond to guest complaints or conflicts promptly. Timely communication shows that you take their concerns seriously and are committed to finding a resolution.

4. Private Communication: Whenever possible, address guest issues privately through direct messages or phone calls. Avoid discussing sensitive matters publicly on your listing page or review section.

5. Find Common Ground: Look for areas of agreement or mutual understanding with the guest. Finding common ground can help build rapport and create a more constructive dialogue.

6. Offer Solutions: Present potential solutions or compromises that address the guest's concerns. Be proactive in finding resolution options that meet both parties' needs.

7. Involve Airbnb Support: If the situation escalates or becomes difficult to resolve, involve Airbnb support to mediate the conflict. They can provide an unbiased perspective and help find a fair resolution.

8. Document Communication: Keep a record of all communication with the guest to ensure clarity and transparency in case further assistance is needed.

9. Set Boundaries: While striving to resolve conflicts, also set clear boundaries for acceptable behavior. Maintain professionalism and enforce your house rules to protect your property and other guests' experiences.

10. Learn from Feedback: View conflicts as opportunities for growth and improvement. Use guest feedback to identify potential areas for enhancement in your listing or hosting practices.

11. Review and Adjust Policies: After resolving a conflict, review your policies and procedures. If necessary, make adjustments to prevent similar issues in the future.

12. Focus on the Positive: Despite challenges, continue providing exceptional service to your other guests. A positive and attentive hosting approach can often mitigate potential conflicts.

9b. Managing Property Maintenance And Cleanliness

Effectively managing property maintenance and cleanliness is essential for providing a delightful guest experience and ensuring the success of your Airbnb business. Here's an original approach to achieve this:

1. Regular Inspections: Conduct regular inspections of your property to identify any maintenance needs or cleanliness issues. Addressing them promptly helps maintain a well-kept space for guests.

2. Preventive Maintenance: Implement a preventive maintenance schedule to address potential problems before they escalate. Regularly service appliances, HVAC systems, and plumbing to minimize unexpected disruptions.

3. Cleaning Checklist: Create a comprehensive cleaning checklist for your property. This ensures that all areas are thoroughly cleaned and sanitized between guest stays.

4. Professional Cleaning Services: Consider hiring professional cleaning services to ensure high-quality and consistent cleanliness. Professional cleaners have expertise in maintaining a spotless environment for guests.

5. Guest Feedback: Encourage guest feedback on cleanliness and maintenance aspects of your property. Utilize their input to improve your

cleaning processes and address any issues proactively.

6. Clear House Rules: Set clear house rules regarding cleanliness expectations for guests. Communicate these rules in your listing and welcome message to ensure guests understand their responsibilities.

7. Timely Repairs: Address maintenance issues reported by guests promptly. Quick and efficient repairs demonstrate your commitment to guest satisfaction and safety.

8. Supply Management: Keep essential cleaning supplies stocked and readily available for guests. Consider providing amenities such as extra towels, linens, and toiletries for their convenience.

9. Exterior Maintenance: Pay attention to the exterior of your property as well. Maintain curb appeal with well-kept landscaping and clean common areas.

10. Team Communication: If you have a team managing your property, maintain open communication channels to relay maintenance and cleaning updates effectively.

11. Seasonal Preparations: Prepare your property for seasonal changes, such as winterizing during colder months or ensuring proper ventilation during summer.

12. Training and Standards: Provide training for your cleaning staff or team to meet your standards for cleanliness and attention to detail. Consistent and meticulous cleaning practices elevate the guest experience.

By adopting this original approach to managing property maintenance and cleanliness, you create a welcoming and hygienic environment for guests. Consistent upkeep and proactive maintenance enhance guest satisfaction, contribute to positive reviews, and foster guest loyalty, ultimately ensuring the continued success of your Airbnb business.

9c. Mitigating Risks Associated With Insurance And Liability

Mitigating risks associated with insurance and liability is crucial to protect your Airbnb business and personal assets. Here's an original approach to achieve this:

1. Comprehensive Insurance Coverage: Invest in comprehensive short-term rental insurance that covers your property, contents, and liability. Verify that your policy explicitly addresses short-term rental activities to ensure adequate protection.

2. Review Insurance Policies: Regularly review your insurance policies to confirm they align with the current needs and size of your Airbnb business. Update coverage as necessary to reflect any changes or expansions.

3. Umbrella Liability Policy: Consider purchasing an umbrella liability policy to provide an extra layer of coverage beyond your standard insurance limits. This protects your assets in case of significant liability claims.

4. Host Protection Programs: Enroll in Airbnb's Host Protection Program or any similar platforms' insurance options to take advantage of additional coverage offered for certain risks associated with hosting.

5. Guest Verification: Implement guest verification procedures to ensure guests' identities are confirmed before check-in. This can help prevent potential issues and ensure a safer hosting environment.

6. Safety Measures: Take proactive steps to enhance guest safety on your property. Install smoke detectors, fire extinguishers, and safety railings where needed to reduce the risk of accidents.

7. Clear House Rules: Set clear house rules that address potential liability concerns, such as pool safety, restricted access areas, or guidelines for using amenities.

8. Property Inspections: Regularly inspect your property to identify and address any safety hazards or maintenance issues that may pose liability risks.

9. Legal Entity Formation: Consider forming a legal entity, such as an LLC (Limited Liability Company), to protect your personal assets in case of lawsuits or claims related to your Airbnb business.

10. Guest Communication: Communicate clearly with guests about potential risks or hazards in and around your property. Provide safety guidelines and emergency contact information for their reference.

11. Indemnification Clauses: Consult with legal professionals to include indemnification clauses in your rental agreements. These clauses can help limit your liability for guest actions or damages.

12. Periodic Risk Assessment: Conduct periodic risk assessments to identify potential hazards and liability concerns. Implement measures to minimize these risks and safeguard your business.

By adopting this original approach to mitigating insurance and liability risks, you can protect your Airbnb business from potential financial setbacks and safeguard your personal assets. Prioritizing safety, adhering to legal guidelines, and maintaining proper insurance coverage contribute to a secure hosting environment and ensure the longevity and success of your hosting venture.

* * *

CHAPTER 10: LONG-TERM SUCCESS AND FUTURE TRENDS

10a. Staying Competitive In The Evolving Airbnb Landscape

Staying competitive in the evolving Airbnb landscape requires adaptability and innovation. Here's an original approach to maintain your competitive edge:

1. Constant Market Analysis: Continuously monitor the Airbnb market in your area to stay updated on trends, demand fluctuations, and competitor strategies. This knowledge helps you make informed decisions and adapt your offerings accordingly.

2. Guest-Centric Approach: Prioritize guest satisfaction and go the extra mile to exceed their expectations. Personalized touches and exceptional hospitality leave a lasting impression and encourage positive reviews and repeat bookings.

3. Unique Selling Proposition: Identify and emphasize the unique features of your property or hosting style. Showcase what sets you apart from other listings, creating a distinctive selling point that attracts guests.

4. Technology Integration: Embrace technology to streamline your operations and enhance the guest experience. Utilize smart locks, automated messaging, and digital check-ins to offer convenience and efficiency.

5. Diverse Listing Options: Consider diversifying your listing options, such as offering entire homes, private rooms, or shared spaces. Catering to different traveler preferences expands your potential guest base.

6. Sustainable Practices: Implement sustainable practices in your property, such as energy-efficient appliances, recycling programs, or eco-friendly amenities. Increasingly, guests value environmentally conscious accommodations.

7. Competitive Pricing: Analyze market rates and adjust your pricing strategy accordingly. Offer competitive rates based on demand, seasonality, and the value you provide to guests.

8. Online Visibility: Optimize your online presence through search engine optimization (SEO), professional photography, and engaging listing descriptions. A strong online presence increases your visibility and attracts more potential guests.

9. Guest Reviews and Testimonials: Encourage satisfied guests to leave positive reviews and testimonials. Positive feedback builds credibility and trust among potential guests.

10. Responsive Communication: Respond promptly to guest inquiries and messages. Quick and attentive communication demonstrates your commitment to excellent customer service.

11. Guest Loyalty Program: Implement a guest loyalty program that rewards repeat guests with discounts or special perks. Encouraging guest loyalty builds a loyal customer base and increases repeat bookings.

12. Continuous Improvement: Embrace a culture of continuous improvement in your Airbnb business. Regularly seek feedback from

guests, analyze performance metrics, and implement enhancements to elevate your hosting standards.

By embracing this original approach to staying competitive in the evolving Airbnb landscape, you position yourself as a sought-after host, attract more bookings, and build a reputable brand. Adapting to changing guest preferences, leveraging technology, and delivering exceptional guest experiences contribute to the ongoing success of your Airbnb business

10b. Leveraging Technology And Automation For Efficiency

Leveraging technology and automation can significantly enhance the efficiency and effectiveness of your Airbnb business. Here's an original approach to make the most of technology:

1. Automated Messaging: Utilize automated messaging systems to promptly respond to guest inquiries, send check-in instructions, and provide essential details about their stay. This streamlines communication and saves time.

2. Smart Locks and Keyless Entry: Install smart locks or keyless entry systems to allow guests to check-in and check-out seamlessly. It eliminates the need for physical keys and enables remote access control for added convenience.

3. Channel Management Software: Invest in channel management software that synchronizes bookings and availability across multiple platforms. This prevents double bookings and simplifies calendar management.
4. Dynamic Pricing Tools: Implement dynamic pricing tools that analyze market demand, competitor rates, and seasonal trends to optimize your

pricing strategy automatically.

5. Property Management Software: Utilize property management software to centralize and organize tasks like guest data, housekeeping schedules, maintenance requests, and financial records.

6. Virtual Tours: Offer virtual tours of your property through 360-degree photos or videos. Virtual tours enable guests to explore your listing remotely and make informed booking decisions.

7. Online Check-In: Enable online check-in options for guests to complete necessary documentation and payment in advance, expediting their arrival process.

8. Digital Guidebooks: Create digital guidebooks with local recommendations, house rules, and essential information for guests to access conveniently on their smartphones.

9. Review Management Tools: Use review management tools to monitor and respond to guest reviews across various platforms. Engaging with reviews demonstrates your commitment to guest satisfaction.

10. Online Payments: Implement secure online payment systems to simplify the booking and payment process for guests. This ensures smooth transactions and reduces the risk of payment delays.

11. Automated Reviews and Feedback: Send automated review requests to guests after their stay. Promptly gathering feedback helps you identify areas for improvement and encourages positive reviews.

12. Data Analytics: Analyze data from your hosting operations to gain insights into guest preferences, booking patterns, and the overall performance of your Airbnb business. Data-driven decisions lead to better outcomes.

By adopting this original approach to leveraging technology and automation, you streamline your Airbnb business, save time, and enhance the guest experience. Embracing modern tools and solutions positions you as a tech-savvy host, attracting more bookings and contributing to your business's long-term success.

10c. Embracing Sustainability And Responsible Hosting Practices

Embracing sustainability and responsible hosting practices for your Airbnb business not only benefits the environment but also enhances the guest experience. Here's an original approach to incorporate sustainability:

1. Eco-Friendly Amenities: Provide eco-friendly amenities, such as biodegradable toiletries, refillable soap dispensers, and reusable water bottles, to reduce single-use plastic waste.

2. Energy Efficiency: Install energy-efficient appliances, LED lighting, and smart thermostats to minimize energy consumption and lower your property's carbon footprint.

3. Waste Reduction: Implement recycling and composting programs to reduce waste generation. Educate guests about waste separation and disposal guidelines.

4. Local and Organic Products: Support local businesses and farmers by offering locally sourced and organic products, including snacks, beverages, and toiletries.

5. Green Transportation Options: Encourage guests to use public transportation or provide bike rentals to promote green transportation alternatives.

6. Water Conservation: Implement water-saving measures, such as low-flow faucets and showerheads, and encourage guests to be mindful of water usage during their stay.

7. Sustainable Cleaning Practices: Use eco-friendly cleaning products that are safe for the environment and guests. Opt for washable and reusable cleaning supplies whenever possible.

8. Nature-Friendly Landscaping: Create a nature-friendly landscape with native plants that require less water and maintenance. Avoid the use of harmful pesticides and herbicides.

9. Educate Guests: Share information about your sustainability initiatives with guests. Provide tips on how they can be environmentally conscious during their stay and when exploring the local area.

10. Digitalization: Minimize paper waste by offering digital check-in instructions, local recommendations, and guest manuals accessible on guests' devices.

11. Donation Programs: Encourage guests to donate any unused or unopened items (such as food or toiletries) to local charities or food banks.

12. Social Responsibility: Get involved in community initiatives and support causes related to sustainability, social welfare, or environmental preservation.

By adopting this original approach to sustainability and responsible hosting practices, you contribute positively to the environment and inspire guests to be conscious travelers. Embracing sustainable practices not only aligns with responsible tourism but also sets your

Airbnb business apart as a responsible and caring host, appealing to eco-conscious guests and enhancing your property's overall reputation.

Conclusion:

"Airbnb Success Awaits: The Blueprint For A Lucrative Startup" provides you with the knowledge, strategies, and inspiration needed to launch and thrive in your own Airbnb business. By following the insights and guidance within this book, you'll be equipped to create exceptional guest experiences, generate significant income, and build a successful and fulfilling entrepreneurial journey in the dynamic world of Airbnb. Start your journey today and unlock the unlimited potential of the sharing economy!

And as an added bonus, scan the QR code below and get 10% off all t-shirt purchases. Simply apply the code BOOK at checkout.